WOULD YOU DARE
SAIL AROUND
THE WORLD?

By Siobhan Sisk

HOT
TOPICS

Gareth Stevens
PUBLISHING

Please visit our website, www.garethstevens.com. For a free color catalog of all our high-quality books, call toll free 1-800-542-2595 or fax 1-877-542-2596.

Cataloging-In-Publication Data

Names: Sisk, Siobhan.
Title: Would you dare sail around the world? / Siobhan Sisk.
Description: New York : Gareth Stevens Publishing, 2017. | Series: Would you dare? | Includes index.
Identifiers: ISBN 9781482458268 (pbk.) | ISBN 9781482458282 (library bound) | ISBN 9781482458275 (6 pack)
Subjects: LCSH: Sailing--Juvenile literature. | Voyages around the world--Juvenile literature.
Classification: LCC GV811.S57 2017 | DDC 797.1'24--dc23

First Edition

Published in 2017 by
Gareth Stevens Publishing
111 East 14th Street, Suite 349
New York, NY 10003

Designer: Laura Bowen
Editor: Therese Shea

Photo credits: Cover, p. 1 (sailing) Lloyd Images/Getty Images Sport/Getty Images; cover, pp. 1–32 (background) Nik Merkulov/Shutterstock.com; cover, pp. 1–32 (paint splat) Milan M/Shutterstock.com; cover, pp. 1–32 (photo frame) Milos Djapovic/ Shutterstock.com; p. 5 Kletr/Shutterstock.com; p. 7 (ship) nbnserge/Shutterstock.com; p. 7 (Magellan) Dantadd/Wikimedia Commons; p. 9 Anri Gor/Shutterstock.com; p. 11 (ship) Monkik/Shutterstock.com; pp. 11, 17 (ocean) Tracy ben/Shutterstock.com; p. 12 Federico Rostango/Shutterstock.com; p. 13 Darren Pierse Kelly/Shutterstock.com; p. 14 Markappa/Wikimedia Commons; p. 15 Shipjustgotreal/Shutterstock.com; p. 17 Radu Bercan/Shutterstock.com; p. 18 Nina B/Shutterstock.com; p. 19 STF/AFP/ Getty Images; p. 21 Greg Dale/National Geographic/Getty Images; p. 23 MARCEL MOCHET/AFP/Getty Images; p. 25 Kos Picture Source/Getty Images Sport/ Getty Images; p. 27 DAMIEN MEYER/AFP/Getty Images; p. 29 AFP/Stringer/ Getty Images; p. 30 Jose Lledo/Shutterstock.com.

Printed in China

CPSIA compliance information: Batch #CW17GS: For further information contact Gareth Stevens, New York, New York at 1-800-542-2595.

CONTENTS

Are You Ready? 4

The First? 6

Different Time, Same Dangers 8

The Sailboat 10

Where to Sail 16

When to Sail 20

Get Packing 22

Crew or Solo? 24

Sailing Records 26

For More Information 31

Glossary 32

Index 32

ARE YOU READY?

Imagine being in a boat on the ocean. There's no land in sight. You can see storm clouds far off. You might see shark fins in the water, too! There's danger as well as wonderful sights when sailing around the world.

DARING DATA

Measured at the middle, it's about 24,900 miles (40,075 km) around Earth.

5

THE FIRST?

Many people think Ferdinand Magellan was the first person to circumnavigate, or sail around, the world. He set sail in September 1519. However, he was killed on the journey. One of his ships completed the journey in September 1522, though.

copy of
Magellan's ship

Ferdinand Magellan

DARING DATA

Many historians think Magellan's slave Enrique
was the first person to truly circumnavigate the world.

DIFFERENT TIME, SAME DANGERS

Sailing around the world today is much different than in Magellan's time. Yet some of the same dangers remain. Storm waves can harm boats. Sicknesses can turn deadly without a doctor's care. And there are still pirates in parts of the world!

DARING DATA

A pirate is someone who attacks and steals from a ship. Pirate attacks happen most often around the coasts of Africa and the Middle East.

9

THE SAILBOAT

A sailboat is a boat whose main power comes from the use of sails. A sailor steers, or directs, the boat by moving the tiller, which moves the rudder in the water. A keel at the boat's bottom keeps it from tipping over.

SAILBOAT PARTS

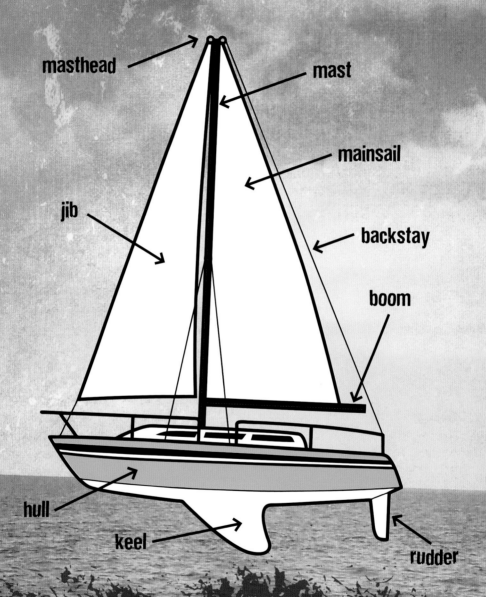

masthead

mast

mainsail

jib

backstay

boom

hull

keel

rudder

DARING DATA

Sailors point the mainsail **perpendicular** to the wind to move the sailboat forward.

Sailing with the wind is easy.
Steering against the wind
is much harder. In fact, it's
impossible to move forward
that way. So sailors sail the
boat at an angle to the wind.
They move forward in a
zigzag path.

DARING DATA

Turning a ship or boat so that the wind is
coming at it from the opposite side is called tacking.

Some fast sailboats have a top speed of more than 45 miles (72 km) an hour. You want your boat to be strong and comfortable, too. The fastest trips around the world take a few weeks. Others take more than a year!

DARING DATA

Sailors often record speed using a measurement called knots. One knot is 1.15 miles (1.85 km) per hour.

WHERE TO SAIL

There are two routes, or paths, most often used to circumnavigate the world (see page 17). Racers use one to circle the globe in the fastest possible time. The other route takes sailors through the Suez and Panama **Canals** and past beautiful sights and popular harbors.

SAILING ROUTES

Europe

Asia

North
America

Suez
Canal

Panama
Canal

Africa

South
America

Atlantic
Ocean

Indian
Ocean

Pacific
Ocean

DARING DATA

The slower route (shown in red) follows the trade winds, which
are winds blowing toward the **equator** from an easterly direction.

Before you leave, there's a lot to study. You need to know about ocean currents and about winds that could slow down or speed up your boat. You also need to know about dangerous areas for sailing.

Cape Horn

DARING DATA

Cape Horn, at the southern end of South America, is known for its rough waters and winds—and shipwrecks!

19

WHEN TO SAIL

Timing is also important when planning your route around the world. For example, strong windstorms called hurricanes strike the Caribbean most often from June to November. Hurricane-strength winds can easily rip sails or cause a boat to capsize, or overturn.

DARING DATA

Reeling the mainsail means cutting down
its area. It makes the boat easier to handle.

GET
PACKING

While you can stop at places along the way, you'll still need to pack well for your journey. You'll need food that won't go bad and plenty of water. You'll need **navigation** tools, too. Don't forget sunscreen!

DARING DATA

You need to have a **passport** and other important papers to stop in most countries.

23

CREW OR SOLO?

Sometimes a team works together to navigate the world. They take turns taking care of the boat and resting. Others are more daring and go on the journey solo, or alone. They have to do all tasks and solve all problems.

DARING DATA

You'll need cold-weather and hot-weather clothes. You don't want to become ill on the high seas!

SAILING
RECORDS

In 2012, a crew set a record for the fastest circumnavigation in a **yacht**, doing it in just 45 days. Frenchman Francis Joyon completed the trip solo in 2008 in 57 days. Both these records were set with trimarans, sailboats with three hulls.

DARING DATA

In 2013, French sailor François Gabart circumnavigated the world in a single-hull boat in 78 days.

Francis Joyon's trimaran

27

Sixteen-year-old Laura Dekker of the Netherlands is the youngest to sail solo around the world. She's been sailing since she was 6! Sailing has its dangers, but with smart preparation, it's one of the best ways to see the world. Would you dare?

DARING DATA

Some people sail the world by **volunteering** on ships.

Laura Dekker

TALK LIKE A SAILOR

SKIPPER – the person in charge of the boat, usually steers it

AFT / STERN – back of the boat

BOW – front of the boat

STARBOARD – right side of the boat when facing bow

PORT – left side of the boat when facing bow

IN IRONS – when the boat is going upwind and can't catch wind in its sails

TRIM SAILS – set sails to catch the wind in the best way

FOR MORE INFORMATION

BOOKS

Klein, Adam G. *Boating*. Edina, MN: ABDO Publishing, 2008.

Teitelbaum, Michael. *Sailing*. Mankato, MN: The Child's World, 2012.

Yomtov, Nelson. *Ferdinand Magellan Sails Around the World*. Minneapolis, MN: Bellwether Media, 2016.

WEBSITES

How Sailboats Work
adventure.howstuffworks.com/outdoor-activities/water-sports/sailboat.htm
Find out how a sailboat works and if you have what it takes to be a sailor.

Sailing Basics: 10 Nautical & Sailing Terms to Know
www.discoverboating.com/resources/article.aspx?id=243
Discover the meaning of many more sailing words.

GLOSSARY

canal: a long, narrow place created by people and filled with water so that boats can pass through it

equator: an imaginary line around Earth that is the same distance from the North and South Poles

navigation: the act of finding the way to get to a place

passport: official papers given by a country's government that state that someone is a citizen of that country

perpendicular: exactly upright or standing at right angles

volunteer: to work without pay

yacht: a sailboat used for racing or pleasure

INDEX

Dekker, Laura 28
Enrique 7
Gabart, François 26
Joyon, Francis 26
keel 10
knots 15

Magellan, Ferdinand 6, 7, 8
mainsail 11, 21
navigation tools 22
pirates 8, 9
rudder 10

routes 16, 17, 20
sails 10, 20
tacking 13
tiller 10